Introducing predators

A true predator is an animal that kills and feeds on another animal. An apex predator is at the top of its food chain and has no natural predators, but it may be hunted by humans or affected by human activity. There are four stages to hunting: finding prey (and also avoiding dangerous prey), attack, capture and eating. The purpose of hunting is to provide enough food to survive and feed young.

To hunt larger prey, gray wolves work in packs of 7 to 8 animals.

A cheetah uses its incredible speed to chase and catch its prey.

A bald eagle uses its daggerlike talons to grab prey.

Characteristics of predators

To be a successful hunter an animal must have highly tuned senses, like excellent vision, taste, hearing, touch and smell, or organs that detect heat, pressure, vibration and more.

They also have to be able to catch their food. This may be through ambush, filtering, venom, shock or trickery (camouflage, mimicry, lures or traps); or by being faster, stronger, more agile and smarter.

A hunter also needs limbs or appendages to manipulate prey and the means (for example, teeth or digestive juices) to consume it.

How to use this book

This book gives you essential facts and informative features on 118 of the animal world's top predators.

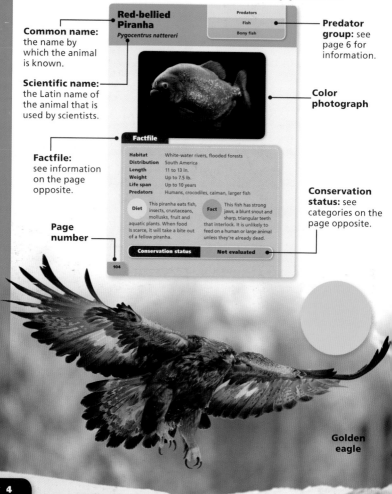

Common name: the name by which the animal is known.

Scientific name: the Latin name of the animal that is used by scientists.

Factfile: see information on the page opposite.

Page number

Predator group: see page 6 for information.

Color photograph

Conservation status: see categories on the page opposite.

Red-bellied Piranha
Pygocentrus nattereri

Predators
Fish
Bony fish

Factfile

Habitat	White-water rivers, flooded forests
Distribution	South America
Length	11 to 13 in.
Weight	Up to 7.5 lb.
Life span	Up to 10 years
Predators	Humans, crocodiles, caiman, larger fish

Diet This piranha eats fish, insects, crustaceans, mollusks, fruit and aquatic plants. When food is scarce, it will take a bite out of a fellow piranha.

Fact This fish has strong jaws, a blunt snout and sharp, triangular teeth that interlock. It is unlikely to feed on a human or large animal unless they're already dead.

Conservation status	Not evaluated

104

Golden eagle

Factfile

The Factfiles provide six key facts and figures about each predator, including where it lives and what it eats.

Habitat
This is the environment in which the predator lives, breeds and hunts.

Distribution
This is the continent, country or ocean where the predator is found.

Size, Length, Height or Wingspan
The predator's dimensions.

Weight
The predator's weight.

Nest size
Where relevant, this is the number of animals found in a nest or colony.

Life span
This tells how long the predator lives, expressed as a range or average.

Predators
This lists the animals that hunt the adult predator. If the young are prey, this is stated. "No natural predators" means the animal is an apex predator.

Diet A brief description of the foods that the predator hunts, forages or scavenges for and eats.

Fact This highlights fascinating information about the predator, like how it hunts and how it eats its prey.

Conservation status

Each animal in this book has been given a conservation status. This status indicates the threat of extinction to the species in its native home.

Not evaluated
The animals within this category have not yet been evaluated for their conservation status.

Least concern
This is the lowest risk category. Animals in this category are widespread and abundant.

Near threatened
The animals in this category are likely to become endangered in the near future.

Vulnerable
There is a high risk that animals within this category will become endangered in the wild.

Endangered
There is a high risk that animals within this category will become extinct in the wild.

Critically endangered
There is an extremely high risk of animals in this category becoming extinct in the wild.

Predator groups

In this book we have divided a selection of prime predator animals into four vertebrate groups – birds, mammals, reptiles and fish – and one wide-ranging invertebrate group.

Reptiles

Reptiles well deserve their cold-blooded, predatory reputation. We have all seen films where a crocodile lunges from the water, grabs an antelope from the bank in its jaws and drags it to a watery death, or a snake slowly swallows its still-warm prey.

Birds

It is not only sharp-taloned, sharp-eyed raptors (birds of prey) with acclaimed hunting skills, there are also canny seabirds and patient wading birds. Not all prey, though, are furred or scaled. Insects, large and very small, and agricultural pests are the bulk of their diet.

Fish

Because sharks will take human prey they often represent the ultimate hunter, but there are many other fish that top their food chain. Take the giant grouper that successfully hunts sharks, and the lionfish that ambushes its prey, cornering it within its venomous spines.

Mammals

Of all the vertebrate (backboned) animals, the hunting prowess of apex mammals like lions, tigers, bears, wolves, whales and seals are the most famed, but the shrewdness, speed and savagery of mammal predators like wild dogs, weasels, fossas, foxes and monkeys are equally effective.

A leopard seal has a large jaw and 1 in. long canine teeth.

A Nile crocodile powers from the water to grab a wildebeest.

Invertebrates

The invertebrate category in this book contains land- and marine-based animals that do not have backbones. It includes insects (the largest and most diverse and successful group of animals on the planet), spiders, soft-bodied mollusks and a small crustacean with a hard external skeleton. The range of hunting techniques employed by these highly adapted animals is truly ingenious.

A jumping spider grasps its prey and injects a fast-acting venom.

Contents

Peregrine Falcon

Falco peregrinus

Predators

Birds

Raptors

Factfile

Habitat	Coasts, forests, deserts, grasslands, heathlands
Distribution	Worldwide (except Antarctica)
Length	14 to 19 in. (body), 32 to 47 in. (wingspan)
Weight	1.1 to 3.3 lb.
Life span	Up to 17 years
Predators	Gyrfalcons, eagles, owls, other peregrines

Diet The peregrine falcon snatches its prey of songbirds, pigeons, starlings, ducks and bats in midair. It also hunts rabbits, rodents, reptiles and fish.

Fact This falcon is the fastest-flying bird in the world, diving at speeds of 155 mph. Adapted to cities, it nests in tall buildings and mates for life.

Conservation status   **Least concern**

Steller's Sea Eagle

Haliaeetus pelagicus

Factfile

Habitat	Coasts, estuaries, rivers, lakeshores, forests
Distribution	Eastern Russia, Japan, eastern China, Korea
Length	33 to 41 in. (body), 8 ft. (wingspan)
Weight	13 to 20 lb.
Life span	Up to 17 years
Predators	No natural predators

Diet This eagle mostly hunts from perches along coasts and lakes for salmon, crabs, squid, ducks, gulls and carrion. It will steal food from other birds.

Fact More aggressive and powerful than the white-tailed sea and bald eagles, this raptor is revered in Japan. It is called *O-washi*, meaning "great eagle."

Conservation status   **Vulnerable**

9

Red-tailed Hawk

Buteo jamaicensis

Predators

Birds

Raptors

Factfile

Habitat	Deserts, grasslands, woodlands, rain forests
Distribution	North and Central America
Length	19 to 25.5 in. (body), 3.5 to 4.5 ft. (wingspan)
Weight	1.8 to 2.5 lb.
Life span	Up to 21 years
Predators	Great horned owls, raccoons, red foxes

Diet These sharp-eyed birds hunt in open areas from adjacent perches (even telephone poles), for mice, birds, ground squirrels, rabbits and reptiles.

Fact The red-tailed hawk is highly aggressive when defending its territory and its nest. It will chase off other hawks and eagles and great horned owls.

Conservation status **Least concern**

Harris's Hawk
Parabuteo unicinctus

Factfile

Habitat	Deserts, grasslands, scrub forests
Distribution	USA, Mexico, Central and South America
Length	18 to 23 in. (body), 3.5 to 4 ft. (wingspan)
Weight	1.1 to 3.5 lb.
Life span	Up to 15 years
Predators	Great horned owls, coyotes, common ravens

Diet Harris's hawks hunt as a team, herding prey and waiting for the moment to strike. They eat medium-sized mammals and birds and reptiles.

Fact These social hawks form units of several individuals. They will hunt, nest and raise young cooperatively, and care for and feed each other if injured.

Conservation status	**Least concern**

Martial Eagle

Polemaetus bellicosus

Predators

Birds

Raptors

Factfile

Habitat	Savannahs, grasslands, scrub forests
Distribution	Sub-Saharan Africa
Length	31 to 38 in. (body), 6.25 to 8.5 ft. (wingspan)
Weight	6.8 to 13.5 lb.
Life span	14 years (average)
Predators	No natural predators, humans

Diet This raptor will feed on birds, including large storks, hyrax and small antelopes, impala calves, goats, lambs and jackals, snakes and lizards.

Fact Africa's largest eagle is powerful enough to knock a person over. It usually hunts from the air, soaring for hours before swooping down for the kill.

Conservation status   **Vulnerable**

Harpy Eagle

Harpia harpyja

Factfile

Habitat   Rain forests
Distribution   Southern Mexico to central South America
Length   35 to 39 in. (body), 5.5 to 7 ft. (wingspan)
Weight   8.8 to 20 lb.
Life span   25 to 35 years
Predators   Lions, bobcats, humans, other harpy eagles

Diet With its huge feet and talons the harpy eagle preys on sloths, monkeys, porcupines, reptiles and large birds. It hunts in the open and in forests.

Fact One of the largest raptors, it has adapted to hunting in densely packed forests, even taking prey from trees, by having a relatively small wing span.

Conservation status   **Near threatened**

13

Golden Eagle

Aquila chrysaetos

Factfile

Habitat   Deserts, forests, grasslands, swampy forests
Distribution Europe, Asia, northern Africa, North America
Length   30 to 35 in. (body), 6 to 7 ft. (wingspan)
Weight   6.6 to 14.3 lb.
Life span   30 to 50 years
Predators   Wolverines, grizzly bears (young only)

Diet Golden eagles soar and glide until they spot small mammals, birds, reptiles, fish and carrion, then they dive at speed to snatch the prey in their talons.

Fact This "booted" eagle – its feathers extend from its body to its yellow feet – is used in falconry, appears on flags and is revered by many cultures.

Conservation status   **Least concern**

14

Bald Eagle

Haliaeetus leucocephalus

Factfile

Habitat   Deserts, grasslands, forests, mountains
Distribution   North America
Length   28 to 38.5 in. (body), 5.9 to 7.5 ft. (wingspan)
Weight   6.6 to 14.3 lb.
Life span   Up to 20 years
Predators   No natural predators

Diet This eagle hunts fish, birds and rodents and will eat carrion. When soaring – it rarely flaps its wings – it will swoop to steal prey from other birds' claws.

Fact Mating or fighting bald eagles will clasp each other's talons in midair and then tumble and spin to the ground only separating at the last moment.

Conservation status   **Least concern**

15

Crowned Eagle
Stephanoaetus coronatus

Predators

Birds

Raptors

Factfile

Habitat	Forests, mountains, grasslands, farmlands
Distribution	Central and southeastern Africa
Length	31.5 to 35.5 in. (body), up to 5.9 ft. (wingspan)
Weight	6 to 9 lb.
Life span	Up to 15 years
Predators	No natural predators

Diet The long hind talon on each toe means the crowned eagle can kill prey – mostly monkeys – four times its size. The talons break the prey's spine.

Fact The short wings and long rudder-like tail are designed to let this raptor maneuver itself easily through the forest canopy hunting for primates.

Conservation status	**Near threatened**

16

Osprey
Pandion haliaetus

Factfile

Habitat	Rivers, ponds, lakes, marshes, coastal waterways
Distribution	Worldwide (except Antarctica)
Length	21.5 to 25.5 in. (body), 4.5 to 5.5 ft. (wingspan)
Weight	3.3 to 4.4 lb.
Life span	20 to 25 years
Predators	Bald eagles, great horned owls, Nile crocodiles

Diet An osprey dives onto its prey of mostly fish but sometimes rodents, rabbits, amphibians and other birds, from 300 ft. It can carry prey weighing 4.4 lb.

Fact This bird is designed for its job. It has reversible outer toes to help grip its catch, nostrils that close and oily plumage to prevent waterlogged feathers.

Conservation status   **Least concern**

Eurasian Eagle Owl

Bubo bubo

Predators

Birds

Raptors

Factfile

Habitat	Tundra, deserts, savannahs, forests, mountains
Distribution	North Africa, Europe, Middle East, Asia
Length	23 to 28 in. (body), 5 to 6.5 ft. (wingspan)
Weight	3.5 to 9 lb.
Life span	Up to 60 years
Predators	No natural predators

Diet This eagle owl takes its prey mid-flight or on the ground, and it hunts and eats everything from insects to juvenile deer, including other birds of prey.

Fact The Eurasian eagle owl is a stealthy, silent hunter nicknamed the "hit man." Its prey does not know it's being stalked until it's too late.

Conservation status   **Least concern**

18

Great Horned Owl

Bubo virginianus

Factfile

Habitat	Forests, woodlands, deserts, marshes, urban areas
Distribution	North, Central and South America
Length	20 to 23.5 in. (body), 3.9 to 4.9 ft. (wingspan)
Weight	1.6 to 5.5 lb.
Life span	5 to 15 years
Predators	Other owls (adults), crows, raccoons (young only)

Diet This owl will hunt and kill prey, like ospreys, peregrine falcons and other owls larger than itself, but will also feed on insects, rodents and amphibians.

Fact The great horned owl uses its strong talons to cut the spine, killing its prey. Once clenched, it takes a force of 26 lb. to open its talons.

Conservation status   **Least concern**

19

Cape Eagle Owl

Bubo capensis

Predators

Birds

Raptors

Factfile

Habitat	Rocky mountain gorges, wooded gullies
Distribution	Eastern and southern Africa
Length	19 to 23 in. (body), 11 to 14 ft. (wingspan)
Weight	2 to 4 lb.
Life span	Up to 10 years
Predators	Other raptors, snakes

Diet This owl eats small mammals, reptiles, birds, scorpions, frogs and crabs. It swoops from its perch, strikes with its talons and bites the prey's head.

Fact The Cape eagle owl will venture from shoreline to snowline and even into cities where it hunts on doves. It can carry 4 times its own body weight.

Conservation status   **Least concern**

Blakiston's Fish Owl

Bubo blakistoni

Factfile

Habitat	Old wood forests near rivers and lakes
Distribution	Eastern Russia, northeastern China, Japan
Length	23.5 to 28 in. (body), up to 6.5 ft. (wingspan)
Weight	6 to 8.8 lb.
Life span	8 to 15 years (estimated)
Predators	No natural predators

Diet This rare owl hunts amphibians, crayfish, small mammals and fish by stalking them on foot or by snatching them from land or water during flight.

Fact The Blakiston's fish owl is endangered due to loss of habitat, decreasing fish stocks and hunters who target it for ruining the fur of trapped animals.

Conservation status	**Endangered**

Goliath Heron

Ardea goliath

Factfile

Habitat	Coastal and inland lakes, rivers, marshes
Distribution	Africa, Middle East, Indian subcontinent
Length	4 to 5 ft. (body), 6.5 ft. (wingspan)
Weight	9.5 to 10 lb.
Life span	Up to 15 years
Predators	African fish eagles (young only)

Diet This long-legged bird will stand motionless for long periods, waiting for prey that includes fish, amphibians, reptiles, rodents and shrimp.

Fact The goliath heron uses a "jackpot" strategy when hunting, passing up small fish and waiting for larger fish to come.

Conservation status	Least concern

Great Black-backed Gull

Larus marinus

Factfile

Habitat	Coasts, estuaries, inland wetlands, refuse sites
Distribution	Northern hemisphere, sometimes South America
Length	25 to 31 in. (body), 5 to 5.5 ft. (wingspan)
Weight	4 to 4.2 lb.
Life span	Up to 27 years
Predators	Eurasian eagle owls, killer whales, sharks

Diet The black-backed gull is an opportunistic predator that will eat whatever it comes across, from carrion and human garbage to fish, and bird eggs and chicks.

Fact This is the largest gull in the world and it has a reputation for being a bully. It harasses other birds, steals their food and even hunts grebes and puffins.

Conservation status   **Least concern**

South Polar Skua

Stercorarius maccormicki

Factfile

Habitat	Coasts, islands, sometimes inland
Distribution	Antarctica
Length	19.5 to 21.5 in. (body), 4 to 4.5 ft. (wingspan)
Weight	2 to 3.5 lb.
Life span	11 years
Predators	Leopard seals, giant petrels

Diet This skua is a hunter and scavenger. It feeds on fish, mostly Antarctic silverfish, petrel eggs and penguin eggs and chicks. It steals food from other birds.

Fact The south polar skua will chase other birds and harass them into regurgitating, then it will eat the food. It will fly hard and fast at any intruders near its nest.

Conservation status   **Least concern**

Great Skua

Stercorarius skua

Factfile

Habitat	Open oceans, offshore islands (breeding only)
Distribution	Northern Atlantic Ocean
Length	19.5 to 23 in. (body), 3.9 to 4.6 ft. (wingspan)
Weight	2.7 to 4.5 lb.
Life span	15 years (average)
Predators	Raptors, orcas (adults), rats, foxes (young only)

Diet Great skuas use their size and aggression to get what they want – prey, eggs or regurgitated food – from other birds. They also feed on shoaling fish.

Fact This cunning bird has learned to avoid a fulmar's toxic oil-spit when it raids its nests, and that walking, not flying, into tern colonies yields more chicks.

Conservation status   **Least concern**

25

Southern Giant Petrel

Macronectes giganteus

Predators

Birds

Seabirds

Factfile

Habitat	Open oceans, islands (breeding)
Distribution	Antarctica
Length	3 to 3.5 ft. (body), 6 to 6.5 ft. (wingspan)
Weight	6.5 to 17.5 lb.
Life span	Up to 25 years
Predators	No natural predators

Diet The southern giant petrel gets most of its food from scavenging carrion and garbage. It will also hunt for penguins, other birds, krill, fish and squid.

Fact This bird is similar in size to an albatross, and its bill can open whole carcasses. Its nickname, "stinker," relates to the foul liquid it spits at intruders.

Conservation status   **Least concern**

African Lion
Panthera leo

Factfile

Habitat   Open woodland, scrubland, grasslands
Distribution Sub-Saharan Africa
Length   4.5 to 8.5 ft. (head/body), 2.5 to 3.5 ft. (tail)
Weight   265 to 550 lb.
Life span   8 to 18 years
Predators   No natural predators

Diet A pride of lions will stalk and ambush prey such as impala, wildebeest, zebra, giraffe, buffalo, wild hogs, rhinos, hippos and small mammals and reptiles.

Fact When food is scarce the king of the jungle (though females do most of the hunting) will steal kills from hyenas and even attack elephants.

| **Conservation status** | **Vulnerable** |

27

Cougar
Puma concolor

Factfile

Habitat	Forests, deserts, canyons, dense underbrush
Distribution	Western North America, Florida, South America
Length	3 to 5 ft. (head/body), 2 to 3 ft. (tail)
Weight	64 to 220 lb.
Life span	18 to 20 years
Predators	Gray wolves, brown bears, jaguars, alligators

Diet The cougar stalks its prey, such as deer, small animals, insects and domestic livestock, then strikes with its claws ready for the kill. It can leap over 20 ft.

Fact Cougars will conceal the carcass of large prey and eat it over the following days. The cougar doesn't roar; it purrs like a domestic cat.

Conservation status   **Least concern**

Siberian Tiger

Panthera tigris altaica

Factfile

Habitat	Birch forests, mountains
Distribution	Siberia (Russia)
Length	4.5 to 9 ft. (head/body), up to 3.5 ft. (tail)
Weight	Up to 650 lb.
Life span	10 to 15 years
Predators	No natural predators, humans

Diet This tiger will travel far to find food such as elk, deer, moose, wild boar, hares, pikas, salmon and small Asian bears. It can eat up to 60 lb. in a day.

Fact The Siberian tiger is the world's largest cat and also the most powerful. Only very rarely, and not recently, has this tiger been a man-eater.

Conservation status   **Endangered**

Clouded Leopard

Neofelis nebulosa

Factfile

Habitat	Dense tropical forests, jungles
Distribution	Southeast Asia, Himalayas
Length	2.5 to 3.5 ft. (head/body), 2.5 to 3 ft. (tail)
Weight	24 to 66 lb.
Life span	11 to 17 years (in captivity)
Predators	Tigers, leopards, humans

Diet This leopard mostly hunts on the ground for pangolins, birds, squirrels, monkeys, deer and wild boar. Sometimes it waits in trees and leaps onto its prey.

Fact The clouded leopard is the best climber of all the cats. It can climb upside down, hang by its hind legs and descend head first. It can also swim.

Conservation status   **Vulnerable**

Cheetah
Acinonyx jubatus

Factfile

Habitat	Open grasslands
Distribution	Asia, Africa, Iran
Length	3.5 to 5 ft. (head/body), 2 to 2.5 ft. (tail)
Weight	88 to 143 lb.
Life span	10 to 12 years
Predators	Lions, hyenas, eagles, leopards

Diet The cheetah, the fastest animal in the world, hunts gazelles, wildebeest calves, impalas and smaller hoofed animals. It eats its prey quickly or hides it.

Fact Camouflaged in tall grasses while it stalks, a cheetah chases its prey for one minute, knocks it to the ground, then delivers a fatal bite to the neck.

Conservation status	**Vulnerable**

31

Leopard
Panthera pardus

Predators

Mammals

Wild cats

Factfile

Habitat	Rain forests, grasslands, mountains
Distribution	Sub-Saharan Africa, southern Asia
Length	3.5 to 6 ft. (head/body), 3.5 to 4.5 ft. (tail)
Weight	66 to 176 lb.
Life span	10 to 15 years
Predators	Lions, tigers, hyenas (young only)

Diet The leopard's spots camouflage it when eyeing prey like deer, antelope or wild boar from a branch. It is a good swimmer, and will also eat fish and crabs.

Fact This animal is very strong and can carry large prey into trees, where it is less likely to be stolen by hyenas. It has been known to attack people.

Conservation status   **Vulnerable**

Geoffroy's Cat

Leopardus geoffroyi

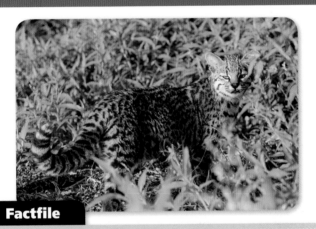

Factfile

Habitat	Savannahs, shrub woodlands, dry forests
Distribution	Southern South America
Length	16 to 26 in. (head/body), 12 in. (tail)
Weight	6.5 to 11 lb.
Life span	14 to 15 years
Predators	No natural predators

Diet Sometimes called the fishing cat, this solitary hunter is opportunistic and feeds on frogs, fish, hares, rodents, birds, lizards and insects.

Fact Unusual among cats, Geoffroy's cat will stand on its hind legs, using its tail as a support, to check its surroundings for prey and predators.

Conservation status   **Least concern**

Caracal
Caracal caracal

Factfile

Habitat	Dry woodlands, savannahs
Distribution	Africa, Asia
Length	2.1 to 3 ft. (body), 7 to 13.5 in. (tail)
Weight	24 to 40 lb.
Life span	12 to 15 years
Predators	Lions, leopards, hyenas

Diet The caracal's diet consists of hyraxes, hares, rodents, birds, antelopes, monkeys and reptiles. Smaller prey are killed with a bite to the neck.

Fact The caracal does not turn away from predators even twice its size, but will chase them down. It will hide larger prey under soil for later eating.

Conservation status   **Least concern**

Serval
Leptailurus serval

Factfile

Habitat	Reed beds, grasslands, forests, thickets, marshes
Distribution	Southern and northern Africa
Length	26 to 39 in. (head/body), 12 in. (tail)
Weight	20 to 40 lb.
Life span	12 to 20 years
Predators	Humans, leopards, hyenas

Diet The serval usually hunts in long grass for birds, rodents and other small mammals, frogs and insects. It will also take to the water for fish.

Fact The serval detects prey with its excellent hearing, uses its height advantage to locate it and its long, powerful legs to pounce on it or leap up to it.

Conservation status   **Least concern**

35

Factfile

Habitat	Hilly and mountainous landscapes, deserts
Distribution	Africa, Arabian Peninsula
Length	20 to 30 in. (head/body), 8 to 14 in. (tail)
Weight	8 to 17.5 lb.
Life span	Up to 15 years
Predators	Foxes, wolves, cats, owls, hawks

Diet The African wild cat's diet is mostly rodents, but it will also eat birds, hares, juvenile antelope or deer, and it eats everything, including the bones.

Fact This wild cat, which can run at speeds of 30 mph, pins its prey to the ground with its claws and then fatally bites or suffocates its prey.

Conservation status   **Least concern**

Leopard Cat
Prionailurus bengalensis

Factfile

Habitat   Forests, scrublands, woodlands near water
Distribution India, southern and eastern Asia
Length   25 to 32 in. (head/body), 10.5 to 14 in. (tail)
Weight   6.5 to 15.5 lb.
Life span   10 to 13 years
Predators   Leopards, tigers, wild dogs, large snakes

Diet This nocturnal hunter takes its prey – mostly rodents, small hoofed animals, birds, reptiles and insects – from the ground and from trees, but it also eats fish.

Fact The leopard cat has webbed toes that helps it swim and scramble up slippery banks. It makes dens in tree hollows and roots and in caves.

Conservation status   **Least concern**

37

Fishing Cat
Prionailurus viverrinus

Factfile

Habitat	Variety of wetland habitats
Distribution	Southeast Asia
Length	22.5 to 33.5 in. (head/body), 8 to 12 in. (tail)
Weight	12 to 17.5 lb.
Life span	10 to 12 years
Predators	No natural predators

Diet The fishing cat eats not just fish, frogs and crustaceans but also young goats, birds, mice, wild dogs and snakes. It will also scavenge carrion.

Fact This cat taps the water to mimic an insect and then uses a webbed paw to scoop up the fish lured to its trap. It also dives for its prey from banks.

Conservation status   **Endangered**

Ocelot
Leopardus pardalis

Factfile

Habitat	Tropical jungles, grasslands, marshes
Distribution	South America
Length	21.5 to 39 in. (head/body), 11 to 18 in. (tail)
Weight	24 to 35 lb.
Life span	8 to 12 years
Predators	Harpy eagles, pumas, jaguars, anacondas

Diet Ocelots hunt rabbits, rodents, iguanas, fish, frogs, young deer, snakes and armadillos. Being agile climbers, they head into trees for birds and monkeys.

Fact Ocelots use pointed fangs to deliver a fatal bite and sharp rear teeth to tear their prey. They cannot chew, so swallow lumps of meat whole.

Conservation status   **Least concern**

Pallas's Cat
Otocolobus manul

Factfile

Habitat   Grasslands, rocky steppes
Distribution Central Asia
Length   20 to 26 in. (head/body), 8 to 12 in. (tail)
Weight   5.5 to 11 lb.
Life span   2.5 years (average)
Predators   Red foxes, corsac foxes, wolves, birds of prey

Diet This cat is an ambush hunter that stalks pikas, small rodents, birds and insects and then pounces on them. It also waits for prey to leave its burrow.

Fact A Pallas's cat is about the same size as a domestic cat, but it appears larger because of the long, dense fur that protects it in its cold habitat.

Conservation status   **Near threatened**

Bobcat
Lynx rufus

Factfile

Habitat   Mountainous forests, deserts, swamps

Distribution   North America

Length   26 to 39 in. (head/body), 7 to 7 in. (tail)

Weight   9 to 33 lb.

Life span   12 to 15 years

Predators   Red foxes, coyotes, large owls, cougars

Diet The bobcat will eat almost anything including rabbits, hares, rodents, birds, bats, beavers, adult deer and domestic livestock.

Fact This cat, recognized by its short tail, hunts from dawn to dusk. It stalks prey often much larger than itself, leaps onto it and inflicts a fatal bite to the neck.

Conservation status   Least concern

Eurasian Lynx

Lynx lynx

Factfile

Habitat	Dense forests, rocky outcrops
Distribution	Central Asia, Europe, Siberia, eastern Asia
Length	2.5 to 4.5 ft. (head/body), 4 to 9.5 in. (tail)
Weight	40 to 79 lb.
Life span	2 to 17 years
Predators	Wolverines, gray wolves, Siberian tigers

Diet The Eurasian lynx climbs trees or high rocks to wait for hoofed mammals, and then leaps down. It kills by choking or suffocating its prey.

Fact This lynx is the largest predator in Europe after the brown bear and gray wolf. Its large webbed paws mean it can run quickly, even in deep, soft snow.

Conservation status   Least concern

Black-footed Cat

Felis nigripes

Factfile

Habitat	Dry grasslands, deserts, sand plains
Distribution	Namibia, Botswana, South Africa
Length	14 to 24 in. (head/body), 8 to 8 in. (tail)
Weight	2.2 to 5.5 lb.
Life span	Up to 13 years
Predators	Wild dogs, caracals, jackals

Diet
This wild cat prefers grassy habitats when hunting as they offer concealment and plenty of rodents and birds. It can catch 12 to 13 prey in a night.

Fact
This is the smallest wild cat and its black-soled feet are insulated from the hot terrain by hair. During the day it hides in abandoned termite mounds.

Conservation status	**Vulnerable**

43

Mandrill
Mandrillus sphinx

Factfile

Habitat	Tropical rain forests, rocky forests, stream beds
Distribution	Nigeria, Cameroon, Gabon, Congo, Equatorial Guinea
Height	1.5 to 2 ft. (on all fours), 2 to 3.5 ft. (standing)
Weight	24 to 72 lb.
Life span	20 years (average)
Predators	Leopards (adults), eagles, pythons (young only)

Diet The mandrill is an omnivore. It eats 100 types of plants and invertebrates and vertebrates. Pouches in its cheeks are used to hold food to consume later.

Fact The mandrill is the largest monkey species. It has long canine teeth that are used both in defense and as a friendly sign to other mandrills.

Conservation status   **Vulnerable**

44

Common Chimpanzee
Pan troglodytes

Factfile

Habitat   Tropical forests, woody savannahs
Distribution Western and central Africa
Height   2 to 3 ft. (on all fours), 3.5 to 5.4 ft. (standing)
Weight   55 to 155 lb.
Life span   50 to 60 years
Predators   Leopards, pythons, crocodiles, humans

Diet The common chimpanzee eats fruits, leaves, honey, insects, other primates and small antelopes. Chimpanzees will often hunt together.

Fact This animal, which is humankind's closest relative, is extinct in four countries and almost extinct in others due to habitat loss and poaching.

Conservation status   **Endangered**

Bonobo
Pan paniscus

Predators

Mammals

Primates

Factfile

Habitat	Tropical forests, swamp forests
Distribution	Democratic Republic of the Congo
Height	11 to 33 in. (on all fours), up to 45 in. (standing)
Weight	66 to 134 lb.
Life span	20 to 50 years
Predators	Crocodiles, humans

Diet The bonobo is an omnivore. Its diet consists of mostly fruit plus leaves, honey, eggs, vertebrates and invertebrates. It will also eat other primates.

Fact This primate spends most of its time on the ground and much of it standing upright. It flees into trees when threatened or when looking for honey.

Conservation status   **Endangered**

Tasmanian Devil

Sarcophilus harrisii

Factfile

Habitat	Coastal scrublands and forests, heaths
Distribution	Tasmania (Australia)
Length	20.5 to 31.5 in.
Weight	9 to 26.5 lb.
Life span	Up to 5 years
Predators	Eagles, owls, large quolls (young only)

Diet This carnivorous marsupial hunts and scavenges for wallabies, small mammals, birds, reptiles, insects and even sea squirts. It also eats carrion.

Fact The screeches and snarls of a Tasmanian devil are terrifying, and like its gaping mouth, usually indicates fear, not a readiness to attack.

Conservation status   **Endangered**

Eurasian Badger
Meles meles

Factfile

Habitat	Woodlands, grasslands, semideserts
Distribution	Europe, Asia, Africa
Length	2 to 3 ft.
Weight	14.5 to 37 lb.
Life span	6 to 14 years
Predators	Humans, wolves, lynxes, bears (young only)

Diet This badger eats earthworms (several hundred a night), insects, frogs, birds, lizards, small mammals, 30 kinds of fruit, eggs, grain and carrion.

Fact The Eurasian badger loves wasp larvae. It rips the top from the nest (to avoid wasps guarding the entrance) and digs through the layers to get to the grubs.

Conservation status   **Least concern**

48

Honey Badger

Mellivora capensis

Factfile

Habitat	Arid grasslands, savannahs, rain forests
Distribution	Africa, Middle East, India
Length	Up to 2.5 ft.
Weight	20 to 26.5 lb.
Life span	Up to 26 years (in captivity)
Predators	Lions, leopards, honeybees, humans

Diet The honey badger's diet includes 60 animal species and plants. It will dig 50 holes a night hunting for prey. It eats bee honeycomb and larvae.

Fact This animal is fearless. It will take on pythons, crocodiles and jackals. Its jaws and teeth can break a tortoise shell. It climbs trees to raid birds' nests.

Conservation status	**Least concern**

49

Wolverine

Gulo gulo

Factfile

Habitat	Dense forests, mountainous regions
Distribution	North America, Europe, Arctic Circle
Length	26 to 34 in. (head/body)
Weight	22 to 68 lb.
Life span	10 to 15 years
Predators	Wolves, mountain lions, bears, humans

Diet This carnivore will hunt and kill small mammals, like rabbits, and large ones, such as caribou. It will eat insects and berries and scavenge carrion.

Fact The bearlike wolverine is the largest land-based weasel. In winter, it will dig into hard or frozen ground to find and eat hibernating prey.

Conservation status   **Vulnerable**

Giant Otter
Pteronura brasiliensis

Factfile

Habitat	Slow-moving rivers, lakes, marshes, flooded land
Distribution	South America (east of the Andes)
Length	5 to 6 ft.
Weight	48.5 to 70.5 lb.
Life span	Up to 12 years
Predators	Jaguars, cougars, anacondas (young only)

Diet This otter hunts for fish, including piranha, but also eats crabs, frogs, snakes, caimans and aquatic mammals. It needs 6 to 9 lb. of food a day.

Fact Known as the "river wolf," the giant otter's whiskers sense changes in current and water pressure, which helps locate prey and detect predators.

Conservation status   **Endangered**

51

Fossa

Cryptoprocta ferox

Factfile

Habitat	Coastal forests and lowlands to mountain areas
Distribution	Madagascar
Length	2 to 2.5 ft. (head/body)
Weight	15.5 to 26.5 lb.
Life span	Up to 17 years
Predators	No natural predators

Diet The fossa mostly hunts in trees for lemurs, its preferred meal, but will also hunt on the ground for frogs, rodents, birds, reptiles and small livestock.

Fact The fossa's tail is as long as its body and helps it balance when leaping through trees. Its claws are retractable, so they are always sharp for hunting.

Conservation status   **Vulnerable**

Small Indian Mongoose

Herpestes javanicus

Factfile

Habitat	Dry forests, scrubland, rain forests
Distribution	Southeast Asia
Length	12 to 26 in. (head/body)
Weight	10.5 to 23 oz.
Life span	Up to 4 years
Predators	Large cobras

Diet The small Indian mongoose feeds on insects, mammals such as rodents, birds, snakes, invertebrates such as crabs, fish, fruit and plant material.

Fact The mongoose's killing method is to bite the back of the prey's head. It has been introduced to island countries to control rats and snakes.

Conservation status	**Least concern**

53

Coyote
Canis latrans

Factfile

Habitat	Forests, mountains, fields, plains, cities
Distribution	North and Central America
Length	29.5 to 35.5 in. (head/body), 16 in. (tail)
Weight	15.5 to 46 lb.
Life span	Up to 15 years
Predators	Wolves, mountain lions, bears, cougars, humans

Diet The coyote has a wide diet: rabbits, insects, fish, frogs, snakes, fruit and livestock. Coyotes living in and around urban areas have the longest life spans.

Fact The speedy coyote has great vision and sense of smell. Small prey is pounced on, while larger prey is tag-chased until exhausted by a coyote pack.

Conservation status	**Least concern**

54

Red Fox
Vulpes vulpes

Factfile

Habitat	Forests, prairies, deserts, mountains, urban areas
Distribution	Northern hemisphere
Length	18 to 35.5 in. (head/body), 12 to 21.5 in. (tail)
Weight	6.5 to 31 lb.
Life span	2 to 4 years
Predators	Eagles, coyotes, wolves, bears, mountain lions

Diet
This fox eats birds, rabbits, rodents, insects, earthworms, berries, fruit, mollusks, frogs, crayfish, reptiles, young lambs, carrion and urban garbage.

Fact
The red fox is highly resourceful and adaptable, able to thrive in almost any habitat. It is listed among the world's top 100 invasive species.

Conservation status   **Least concern**

55

Gray Wolf

Canis lupus

Predators

Mammals

Dogs and relatives

Factfile

Habitat	Tundra, forests, prairies, deserts, mountains
Distribution	Eastern Europe, Russia, North America
Length	41 to 63 in. (head/body), 11 to 20 in. (tail)
Weight	50 to 176 lb.
Life span	5 to 13 years
Predators	Wolves, coyotes (young only)

Diet When hunting alone, a gray wolf can bring down a deer, but a pack can kill caribou, elk and moose. A single gray wolf can eat 20 lb. in one sitting.

Fact This wolf forms strong bonds and will sacrifice itself for the family unit. It feeds its young with regurgitated food, and avoids contact with humans.

Conservation status   Least concern

Maned Wolf

Chrysocyon brachyurus

Factfile

Habitat	Tall grasslands, open forests, marshlands
Distribution	Central-western South America
Length	4 to 4.25 ft. (head/body), 1.5 ft. (tail)
Weight	44 to 51 lb.
Life span	Up to 13 years
Predators	No natural predators

Diet The maned wolf eats wild guinea pigs, rabbits, rodents, insects, reptiles, birds, fruit and plants. It kills with a bite to the head or by shaking.

Fact Nicknamed the "fox on stilts" for its long legs, which help the wolf spot prey in tall grass, it taps the ground with a paw to disturb prey and then pounces.

Conservation status	**Near threatened**

Brown Bear

Ursus arctos

Factfile

Habitat	Forests, woodlands, desert edges to ice fields
Distribution	Northern North America, Europe, Asia
Length	5 to 9 ft.
Weight	300 to 640 lb.
Life span	20 to 30 years
Predators	Other bears, wolves, tigers, cougars, humans

Diet This bear eats grasses in spring, salmon and fruit in summer, and nuts and plums in autumn. Year-round it eats honey, mammals, insects and reptiles.

Fact In autumn, the brown bear doubles its weight, eating 90 lb. of food a day, to ready itself for hibernation. Its forepaw claws measure 2 to 4 inches.

Conservation status   Least concern

American Black Bear

Ursus americanus

Factfile

Habitat	Forests, woodlands, tundra, mountains, swamps
Distribution	North America
Length	4.5 to 6 ft.
Weight	220 to 595 lb.
Life span	15 to 30 years
Predators	Humans (adults), bears, foxes, raptors (young only)

Diet This bear eats plants, fruit, nuts, insects, honey, fish (mostly salmon), small and large mammals and carrion, but most of its diet is plant-based.

Fact The black bear climbs trees and swims. It will enter settlements and campsites looking for food. It can open jars and undo door latches.

Conservation status   **Least concern**

Polar Bear
Ursus maritimus

Predators

Mammals

Bears

Factfile

Habitat   Pack ice, ice floes
Distribution   Arctic region
Length   5 to 8 ft.
Weight   330 to 1322 lb.
Life span   25 to 30 years
Predators   Other polar bears, humans

Diet The bulk of this bear's diet is ringed seal. It is a patient hunter that ambushes a seal at its air hole or stalks it, starting its attack run 22 ft. from the seal.

Fact A polar bear can smell a seal even when it's half a mile away. It is a powerful predator but only one in fifty hunts result in the bear catching a meal.

Conservation status   Vulnerable

Blue Whale

Balaenoptera musculus

Factfile

Habitat	Open oceans
Distribution	Worldwide
Length	Up to 110 ft.
Weight	Up to 395,000 lb.
Life span	60 to 120 years
Predators	No natural predators

Diet This amazing whale feeds on krill, straining it from the water on yard-long baleen plates. During summer it needs to eat 2,000 to 9,000 lb. of krill a day.

Fact The largest animal ever to have lived has two blowholes that can measure 23 in. across and send vapor 40 ft. high. Its tongue weighs 8,800 pounds.

Conservation status   **Endangered**

Sperm Whale

Physeter macrocephalus

Predators

Mammals

Whales

Factfile

Habitat	Deep-water oceans
Distribution	Worldwide (except high Arctic waters)
Length	Up to 62 ft.
Weight	Up to 128,000 lb.
Life span	70 years
Predators	Orcas

Diet The favored food of the toothed sperm whale is deep-water squid. It sucks the squid into its mouth. It has 40 to 52 teeth, each 8 inches long.

Fact This whale has a single, bushy, angled blowhole. A car-sized cavity in its head contains a special oil that aids hearing and deep-dive buoyancy.

Conservation status   **Vulnerable**

Orca
Orcinus orca

Factfile

Habitat	Coastal regions
Distribution	Worldwide
Length	16.5 to 26 ft.
Weight	15,000 to 19,000 lb.
Life span	Up to 90 years (female), 60 years (male)
Predators	No natural predators (adults), sharks (young only)

Diet An orca's diet varies depending on location, but typically they eat whales, fish, sharks, rays, seals, sea turtles, octopuses, seabirds, dolphins and squid.

Fact Orcas earned their nickname "wolves of the sea" because they hunt in organized "packs." It can take several hours for five orcas to hunt down a whale.

Conservation status   **Not evaluated**

Australian
Sea Lion
Neophoca cinerea

Predators

Mammals

Seals

Factfile

Habitat	Oceans, rocky and sandy islands
Distribution	Southern Australia
Length	6 to 8 ft.
Weight	230 to 550 lb.
Life span	Up to 26 years
Predators	Great white sharks, orcas

Diet This sea lion forages at all times of the day, diving to the seabed for cephalopods, fish, crustaceans and occasionally penguins. It also eats seabirds.

Fact The Australian sea lion, the most endangered sea lion in the world, is a powerful, fast swimmer that surprises its prey unawares.

Conservation status   **Endangered**

Leopard Seal

Hydrurga leptonyx

Factfile

Habitat	Pack ice, cold ocean waters
Distribution	Antarctic region
Length	8 to 10.5 ft.
Weight	440 to 1,300 lb.
Life span	20 to 24 years
Predators	Orcas, sharks

Diet The leopard seal feeds on krill, fish, cephalopods, seals, seabirds and penguins. With its large canine teeth, it can eat a penguin in 4 to 7 minutes.

Fact This cunning predator will break through thin ice to snatch a chick from a penguin rookery. It filters krill from the water with specially shaped cheek teeth.

Conservation status   **Least concern**

Mediterranean Monk Seal

Monachus monachus

Predators

Mammals

Seals

Factfile

Habitat	Coastal waters, remote caves
Distribution	Mediterranean Sea, northwestern African coast
Length	Up to 8 ft.
Weight	660 to 695 lbs.
Life span	Up to 30 years
Predators	No natural predators

Diet The Mediterranean monk seal hunts fish, rays, cephalopods and crustaceans. To kill prey, it tosses it in the air, so it lands heavily on water or land.

Fact This seal is the most endangered of all seals due to loss of breeding habitat. It hunts most efficiently in open waters, where it can use its speed.

Conservation status	**Endangered**

Boa Constrictor

Boa constrictor

Factfile

Habitat	Tropical woodlands, scrubland
Distribution	Central and South America
Length	Up to 13 ft.
Weight	Up to 88 lb.
Life span	20 to 30 years
Predators	Jaguars, crocodiles, some large birds, humans

Diet This snake eats large lizards, opossums, squirrels, mongooses, rats and monkeys, but bats are a top prey. It snatches them mid-flight or from their roosts.

Fact The boa's hooked teeth make it impossible for prey to escape once in the snake's jaws. It kills by crushing the prey and swallows it whole.

Conservation status   **Not evaluated**

67

Burmese Python

Python molorus bivittatus

Factfile

Habitat	Grasslands, swamps, woodlands, river valleys
Distribution	Southeast Asia, southern Florida
Length	16.5 to 26 ft.
Weight	Up to 360 lb.
Life span	20 to 25 years
Predators	Alligators, humans

Diet The Burmese python uses constriction to kill mammals, birds and even alligators (Florida). It is often found near towns where rodents are plentiful.

Fact A young python lives in trees, but as an adult, when its girth can equal that of a telephone pole, it lives on the ground.

Conservation status   **Vulnerable**

68

Gaboon Viper
Bitis gabonica

Factfile

Habitat	Rain forests, grasslands, deserts
Distribution	Northwest and eastern Africa
Length	4 to 8 ft.
Weight	Up to 44 lb.
Life span	Up to 18 years
Predators	No known natural predators

Diet This snake lies still until small mammals and birds come near. Then it strikes rapidly, holding the prey in its fangs until it dies.

Fact The Gaboon viper is the world's heaviest venomous snake, and its 2 in. fangs inject the most venom of any snake, certainly enough to kill a human.

Conservation status   **Least concern**

Black Mamba

Dendroaspis polylepis

Predators

Reptiles

Snakes

Factfile

Habitat	Savannahs, tropical forests, rocky hills, near lakes
Distribution	Sub-Saharan Africa
Length	6.5 to 8 ft.
Weight	Up to 3.5 lb.
Life span	Up to 11 years
Predators	Birds of prey, monitor lizards, mongooses, jackals

Diet This mamba is an aggressive predator of amphibians, birds, reptiles, bush babies, rock hyraxes and bats. It will hunt in trees and on the ground.

Fact The black mamba is fast and kills with one or more venomous, paralyzing bites. It releases its fangs and waits for the prey to die, then swallows it whole.

Conservation status   **Least concern**

Eastern Diamondback

Crotalus adamanteus

Factfile

Habitat   Dry pine woods, sandy areas, offshore islands
Distribution Southeastern USA
Length   2.5 to 6 ft.
Weight   2 to 5 lb.
Life span   Up to 20 years
Predators   Eagles, hawks, badgers, kingsnakes

Diet This rattlesnake eats rodents, rabbits, squirrels and birds. Its venom kills red blood cells and breaks down tissue, making the prey easier for it to digest.

Fact The diamondback rattler's needlelike fangs lie flat in its mouth until needed. A 6 foot snake strikes with 4 feet of its body off the ground.

Conservation status	Least concern

71

Brown Tree Snake

Boiga irregularis

Predators

Reptiles

Snakes

Factfile

Habitat	Rain forests, mangroves, forests, urban areas
Distribution	Australia, Indonesia, Papua New Guinea
Length	3.5 to 6.5 ft.
Weight	Up to 5 lb.
Life span	Up to 13 years
Predators	Monitor lizards, feral pigs and cats, cane toads

Diet This tree snake eats birds, eggs, reptiles, frogs and small mammals. It bites its prey, coils around it and then chews the prey to inject more venom.

Fact This snake is the world's most invasive species. Introduced to an island in Micronesia in the 1950s, it almost destroyed the entire native bird population.

Conservation status   Not evaluated

African Rock Python

Python sebae

Factfile

Habitat	Evergreen forests, wet savannahs, rock outcrops
Distribution	Sub-Saharan Africa
Length	10 to 16.5 ft.
Weight	97 to 213 lb.
Life span	Up to 30 years (in captivity)
Predators	African wild dogs, hyenas

Diet This snake ambushes prey such as monkeys, crocodiles, lizards, antelopes and fish. It can bite and constrict an antelope weighing up to 130 pounds.

Fact This snake is a ground dweller but can climb trees and swim. As with other constrictors, it does not crush the prey but restricts its breathing until it dies.

Conservation status	**Not evaluated**

73

King Brown Snake

Pseudechis australis

Factfile

Habitat	Woodlands, grasslands, deserts
Distribution	Australia (except eastern and southern coasts)
Length	5 to 9 ft.
Weight	6.5 to 13 lb.
Life span	20 to 30 years
Predators	Cane toads, birds of prey (young only)

Diet This snake ambushes frogs, birds, small mammals, lizards, invertebrates and carrion. It also eats other snakes, even venomous ones, and eggs.

Fact When cornered, the king brown expands its body, flattens its neck and raises its head. It strikes to bite, then chews the prey to inject more venom.

Conservation status	**Not evaluated**

74

South American Bushmaster

Lachesis muta

Factfile

Habitat   Tropical moist forests
Distribution   Central and South America
Length   6.5 to 12 ft.
Weight   6.5 to 11 lb.
Life span   12 to 18 years (in captivity)
Predators   Humans, other snakes, raptors (young only)

Diet   This large snake ambushes rodents, birds, reptiles and amphibians, and can live on less than 10 large meals a year.

Fact   This bushmaster is a solitary, secretive reptile that hunts at night. A pair of heat-sensitive organs on its face detect when prey is within striking distance.

Conservation status	Not evaluated

Inland Taipan

Oxyuranus microlepidotus

Factfile

Habitat	Hot dry scrubland, deserts, rock outcrops
Distribution	Southwest Queensland, northeastern South Australia
Length	6 to 8 ft.
Weight	6.5 lb.
Life span	10 to 15 years (in captivity)
Predators	King brown snakes, monitor lizards

Diet The inland taipan eats small mammals, especially long-haired rats and house mice. It corners its prey and bites it up to 8 times while it's gripped in its jaws.

Fact Listed as the world's most venomous snake, this taipan is rarely encountered by humans due to its remote location, shyness and daytime inactivity.

Conservation status **Not evaluated**

Komodo Dragon
Varanus komodoensis

Factfile

Habitat	Hot grasslands, tropical dry or wet forests
Distribution	5 islands in southeastern Indonesia
Length	Up to 10 ft.
Weight	Up to 175 lb.
Life span	Up to 50 years
Predators	No natural predators

Diet The dragon eats pigs, water buffalo, insects and other dragons. It lunges on its hind legs, knocks its prey over, then shreds it to pieces with sharklike teeth.

Fact This largest living lizard is muscular and covered with bony plates. It can spot prey 1,000 ft. away, run at speeds of 12 mph and has toxic saliva.

Conservation status **Vulnerable**

Asian Water Monitor

Varanus salvator

Predators

Reptiles

Lizards

Factfile

Habitat   Fresh- and salt water, forests, swamps
Distribution   Southern Asia, Malaysia, Indonesia
Length   5 to 10 ft.
Weight   55 to 110 lb.
Life span   Up to 10 years
Predators   Crocodiles, large snakes, otters, birds of prey

Diet This monitor eats insects, crabs, snakes, mollusks, eggs, fish, eels (up to 3 ft. in length), birds, rodents, other monitor lizards, garbage, feces and carrion.

Fact The water monitor chases or swims after its prey. It can remain underwater for 30 minutes. It finds its prey by scent organs located on its forked tongue.

Conservation status   **Least concern**

78

Crocodile Monitor
Varanus salvadorii

Factfile

Habitat	Coastal lowlands, tropical rain forests, swamps
Distribution	Papua New Guinea, West Papua
Length	6.5 to 16.5 ft.
Weight	44 to 200 lb.
Life span	12 to 20 years
Predators	No natural predators

Diet This lizard hunts birds, rodents, reptiles, amphibians and insects. Its jaw and teeth structure mean it can snatch fast-moving prey.

Fact The crocodile monitor lives on the ground and in trees, where its long tail helps it balance. Unlike other monitors, it can run and breathe at the same time.

Conservation status   **Least concern**

79

Alligator Snapping Turtle

Macrochelys temminckii

Factfile

Habitat	Rivers, canals, lakes, swamps
Distribution	Southeastern USA
Length	14 to 34.5 in.
Weight	50 to 175 lb.
Life span	50 to 100 years
Predators	Humans (adults), raccoons, birds (young only)

Diet
This snapping turtle eats fish, frogs, clams, snakes, snails, worms, crayfish, other turtles and aquatic plants. Once prey is in its mouth, the jaws slam shut.

Fact
Known as the "dinosaur of the turtle world," its tongue is equipped with a wormlike looking "lure." It wriggles it to attract prey.

Conservation status   **Vulnerable**

Leatherback Sea Turtle
Dermochelys coriacea

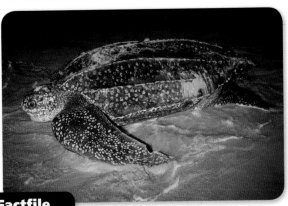

Factfile

Habitat	Open seas
Distribution	Worldwide (except polar oceans)
Length	Up to 5 ft. (carapace length)
Weight	550 to 1,985 lb.
Life span	At least 30 years
Predators	Orcas, sharks

Diet This large turtle eats low-protein squid, jellyfish and tunicates. It must consume twice its body weight in food each day.

Fact Of 1,000 leatherback hatchlings only 1 will survive to adulthood. The eggs are poached, they are caught on longlines and choked by plastic garbage.

Conservation status	**Vulnerable**

81

Saltwater Crocodile

Crocodylus porosus

Predators

Reptiles

Crocodiles, alligators and gharials

Factfile

Habitat	Coastal salt water, fresh and brackish water
Distribution	Australia, southeast Asia, India
Length	Up to 20 ft.
Weight	2,200 to 2,650 lb.
Life span	Up to 70 years
Predators	No natural predators, humans

Diet As this crocodile ages, its diet widens to include crustaceans, turtles, lizards, snakes, birds and larger prey like buffalo, wallabies and wild pigs.

Fact This crocodile stays almost completely submerged until prey is near, then it explodes into action, throwing itself onto banks or through the water.

Conservation status Least concern

Nile Crocodile

Crocodylus niloticus

Factfile

Habitat	Freshwater rivers, marshes, mangroves, swamps
Distribution	Saharan Africa, Nile Basin, Madagascar
Length	Up to 20 ft.
Weight	485 to 2,400 lb.
Life span	Up to 45 years
Predators	No natural predators

Diet The Nile crocodile ambush-hunts fish, zebras, small hippos, birds and other crocodiles. Land-based prey is dragged into the water and drowned.

Fact This crocodile is a social animal and a team of crocodiles will cooperate to herd fish into an area. They will then feed in order of the group's hierarchy.

Conservation status   **Least concern**

83

American Alligator

Alligator mississippiensis

Predators

Reptiles

Crocodiles, alligators and gharials

Factfile

Habitat	Slow-moving freshwater lakes, swamps, marshes
Distribution	Southeastern USA
Length	10 to 15 ft.
Weight	Up to 1,000 lb.
Life span	35 to 50 years
Predators	Bobcats, alligators, birds, raccoons (young only)

Diet This alligator ambush-hunts fish, turtles, frogs, birds, mammals and snakes, but it is not fussy and will eat almost anything including carrion.

Fact Small prey is eaten whole. Larger prey is shaken, gripped in the crocodile's jaws, until small pieces are ripped off.

Conservation status   **Least concern**

False Gharial

Tomistoma schlegelii

Factfile

Habitat	Freshwater swamps, forests, lakes, rivers
Distribution	Indonesia, Malaysia, Brunei
Length	13 to 16.5 ft.
Weight	210 to 460 lb.
Life span	60 to 80 years
Predators	Humans, wild pigs, monitor lizards (young only)

Diet The false gharial is an opportunistic hunter, preying on monkeys, wild pigs, wild dogs, otters, fish, birds, invertebrates, and turtles and other reptiles.

Fact This gharial will lie in wait for prey (almost submerged). An animal snatched from a bank will be drowned or thrown against the bank until dead.

Conservation status   **Vulnerable**

Bull Shark

Carcharhinus leucas

Predators

Fish

Cartilaginous fish

Factfile

Habitat	Shallow warm salt water and freshwater
Distribution	Worldwide
Length	6.9 to 11.2 ft.
Weight	200 to 500 lb.
Life span	16 years
Predators	Tiger sharks, great white sharks, crocodiles

Diet The agile bull shark eats other sharks and fish, turtles, rays, mollusks and seabirds. It first bumps its prey, which may kill or stun it, then it bites.

Fact This shark ranks as the third most-dangerous shark when it comes to attacks on humans. It is unpredictable, territorial and aggressive.

Conservation status   **Near threatened**

86

Great White Shark

Carcharodon carcharias

Factfile

Habitat	Temperate coastal and offshore water
Distribution	Worldwide
Length	Up to 20 ft.
Weight	Up to 4,850 lb.
Life span	70 years
Predators	Orcas

Diet The great white is equipped with 300 serrated teeth and an exceptional sense of smell. It hunts sea lions, seals, toothed whales, sea turtles and carrion.

Fact This is the top-ranked shark for attacks on humans and the largest predatory fish. It torpedoes at speeds up to 35 mph, often from below, to its prey.

Conservation status	**Vulnerable**

Tiger Shark

Galeocerdo cuvier

Predators
Fish
Cartilaginous fish

Factfile

Habitat	Warm shallow and open waters
Distribution	Worldwide
Length	14 to 20 ft.
Weight	850 to 1400 lb.
Life span	30 to 40 years
Predators	No natural predators, humans

Diet With its excellent vision, this shark hunts at night for other sharks and mammals, fish and reptiles. It also swallows tires and boat parts.

Fact This shark ranks high on attacks on humans. In Hawaii, these shallow-water sharks are hunted to reassure tourists. Others are killed by ships and boats.

Conservation status	Near threatened

Marbled Electric Ray

Torpedo sinuspersici

Factfile

Habitat	Tropical sandy shallow waters, reefs
Distribution	Indian Ocean, Persian Gulf, Andaman Sea
Length	Up to 4.25 ft.
Weight	Up to 28.5 lb.
Life span	15 to 20 years
Predators	Occasionally sharks and other large fish

Diet This slow-moving ray ambushes its prey, covering it with its pectoral fins, and then delivers the shock. It preys on seabed fish and invertebrates.

Fact This ray's pair of electrical organs are positioned on the head and can be seen through the skin. It will use shocks when threatened or attacking.

Conservation status   Not evaluated

Giant Grouper
Epinephelus lanceolatus

Predators	
Fish	
Bony fish	

Factfile

Habitat	Shallow-water caves, reefs, estuaries
Distribution	Indo-Pacific region
Length	Up to 9 ft.
Weight	Up to 880 lb.
Life span	Up to 50 years
Predators	Large sharks, humans

Diet This large grouper's preferred prey is crayfish, but it also feeds on small sharks, juvenile sea turtles, fish and crabs. It swallows its meal whole.

Fact The giant grouper is the largest reef dweller in the world, and it is heading to extinction because of its use in medicines and as a food.

Conservation status   **Vulnerable**

Black Grouper

Mycteroperca bonaci

Factfile

Habitat	Shallow-water reefs, estuaries
Distribution	Western Atlantic Ocean
Length	Up to 5 ft.
Weight	Up to 220 lb.
Life span	14 to 30 years
Predators	Sandbar sharks, great hammerheads, moray eels

Diet Black grouper adults feed on fish, squid and crustaceans; the juveniles eat crustaceans. Multiple sets of teeth stop prey escaping once caught.

Fact These fish, taken by fisherman and by commercial trawlers, have a reducing population, so size and catch limits and closed seasons have been introduced.

Conservation status	**Near threatened**

91

Giant Moray Eel

Gymnothorax javanicus

Predators

Fish

Bony fish

Factfile

Habitat	Lagoons and reefs
Distribution	Indo-Pacific region
Length	Up to 10 ft.
Weight	Up to 65 lb.
Life span	3 to 36 years
Predators	Groupers, barracudas, sea snakes

Diet This eel and the coral grouper hunt as a team. The sinuous eel flushes fish or crustaceans from crevices, while the speedy grouper chases them down.

Fact This eel, in common with all moray eels, has very poor eyesight, so it relies on a highly developed sense of smell to find and catch prey.

Conservation status   **Not evaluated**

Electric Eel

Electrophorus electricus

Factfile

Habitat	Muddy bottoms of rivers and swamps
Distribution	Northeastern portions of South America
Length	8 ft.
Weight	Up to 44 lb.
Life span	10 to 22 years
Predators	No natural predators (adults)

Diet This eel uses electrical power, which is stronger than a household power outlet, to stun and paralyze its prey – mostly fish and amphibians.

Fact The electric eel can produce a charge of up to 600 volts, and its body's electric organ contains 6,000 cells that store power in the same way as a battery.

Conservation status	**Least concern**

Great Barracuda

Sphyraena barracuda

Predators
Fish
Bony fish

Factfile

Habitat	Temperate shallow waters and deep reefs
Distribution	Atlantic and Indo-West-Pacific Oceans
Length	2 to 5.5 ft.
Weight	5.5 to 110 lb.
Life span	Up to 14 years
Predators	Sharks, tuna, goliath groupers

Diet This fast-moving predator hunts for fish, cephalopods and shrimp. Its large mouth and razor-sharp teeth means it can cut even large prey in half.

Fact The great barracuda has a streamlined body and fearsome teeth. It sometimes trails divers who have taken its prey, but injury-causing attacks are rare.

Conservation status   **Least concern**

Atlantic Sailfish

Istiophorus albicans

Factfile

Habitat	Shallow warm coastal waters
Distribution	Atlantic Ocean
Length	Up to 11 ft.
Weight	120 to 200 lb.
Life span	4 to 7 years
Predators	Dolphinfish, other large predatory fish, seabirds

Diet Sailfish hunt for fish and cephalopods. It herds a shoal into a "bait ball," then stuns or kills prey with its bill before eating those that can't swim away.

Fact This sail-finned fish can fold its pectoral fins into grooves on its body to help it travel at speeds of 70 mph. Its upper jawbone ends as a pointed bill.

Conservation status	**Not evaluated**

Swordfish

Xiphias gladius

Factfile

Habitat	Warm waters, occasional cold waters
Distribution	Worldwide
Length	Up to 14.5 ft.
Weight	Up to 1200 lb.
Life span	Up to 9 years
Predators	Orcas, sharks, dolphinfish, tuna (young only)

Diet The swordfish uses its bill to strike, thrash, slash and impale its prey, such as fish, squid and octopus. It will eat small prey whole, but slash larger prey.

Fact The bill of a swordfish is half as long as its body. Its eyes are the size of softballs, giving it acute sight. Its flesh is essentially all power-generating muscle.

Conservation status   **Least concern**

White Marlin

Kajikia albida

Factfile

Habitat	Tropical and subtropical oceans
Distribution	Western Atlantic Ocean
Length	Up to 10 ft.
Weight	60 to 180 lb.
Life span	15 years
Predators	No natural predators, humans

Diet This marlin prefers a diet of flying fish, dolphinfish, small tuna and squid. It will cruise with other apex predators to increase foraging success.

Fact The white marlin uses its bill to stun its prey, then turns around to consume it. It dives for food. A long, 75-minute U-shaped dive means the hunt was successful.

Conservation status — **Vulnerable**

97

Giant Trevally

Caranx ignobilis

Predators
Fish
Bony fish

Factfile

Habitat	Tropical water reefs, bays, lagoons, estuaries
Distribution	Pacific and Indian Oceans
Length	Up to 5 ft.
Weight	Up to 175 lb.
Life span	25 years (estimated)
Predators	No natural predators

Diet This fish eats small fish, especially fusiliers, other trevally, crustaceans and cephalopods. It slams into its prey and eats it whole.

Fact The giant trevally is a strong swimmer, able to handle powerful currents and swells. It hunts alone or in groups, and will shadow other fish for its catch.

Conservation status	Not evaluated

Common Lionfish

Pterois volitans

Factfile

Habitat	Tropical reefs and rocky crevices
Distribution	Indo-Pacific region
Length	12 to 16 in.
Weight	Up to 2.5 lb.
Life span	Up to 15 years
Predators	Other lionfish, moray eels, groupers, cornetfish

Diet The lionfish eats fish, crabs, starfish, squid, octopuses and mollusks. Its long spines sweep small fish into a crevice and then the lionfish eats its trapped prey.

Fact This fish has 17 venomous dorsal, pectoral and anal spines. When approached, it holds its ground and points its spines at the intruder.

Conservation status	**Not evaluated**

Northern Pike

Esox lucius

Factfile

Habitat	All freshwater habitats
Distribution	North America, Europe
Length	2.5 to 4 ft.
Weight	Up to 55 lb.
Life span	Up to 12 years
Predators	No natural predators

Diet This pike is an ambush predator with very sharp teeth. It eats smaller fish (even other pike), frogs, crayfish, small mammals, birds and insects.

Fact The northern pike is an aggressive, solitary fish. It attacks with speed in its signature S-pose from its hiding spot. Its eyes can see in almost any direction.

Conservation status   **Least concern**

Smallmouth Bass

Sunfish

Factfile

Habitat	Gravel-bottomed freshwater lakes and streams
Distribution	North America (native), worldwide (introduced)
Length	Up to 27 in.
Weight	Up to 12 lb.
Life span	6 to 14 years (average)
Predators	Other fish, turtles, osprey, kingfishers, humans

Diet
This bass relies on sight and clear water to find and capture prey such as crayfish, other fish and smallmouth bass, amphibians and insects.

Fact
The smallmouth bass is often the apex predator in its habitat. It has been introduced to many countries as a feisty gamefish for anglers.

Conservation status   **Least concern**

101

Wels Catfish

Silurus glanis

Factfile

Habitat	Warm freshwater lakes, deep slow rivers
Distribution	Europe, Asia
Length	Up to 15 ft.
Weight	Up to 660 lb.
Life span	Up to 80 years
Predators	Northern pikes, humans

Diet
The wels catfish eats other fish, crayfish, mussels, rodents and worms. It swims onto shores to catch birds. It sucks prey whole into its large mouth.

Fact
This catfish is a "megafish" because of its size. Some believe the Loch Ness monster is a wels catfish. It hunts at night and its skin is slimy.

Conservation status   **Least concern**

Predators

Fish

Bony fish

Redtail Catfish

Phractocephalus hemioliopterus

Factfile

Habitat	Freshwater rivers, lakes, rapids, flooded forests
Distribution	South America
Length	Up to 6 ft.
Weight	Up to 175 lb.
Life span	Up to 20 years (in captivity)
Predators	Not recorded

Diet This slow-moving, bottom-dwelling fish ambush-hunts mostly other fish, including catfish, and crabs. In flooded forests it will eat fallen fruit and seeds.

Fact This long-whiskered catfish is territorial and aggressive even when young. The whiskers (barbels) contain taste and smell receptors to aid hunting.

Conservation status	**Not evaluated**

Red-bellied Piranha

Pygocentrus nattereri

Predators	
Fish	
Bony fish	

Factfile

Habitat	White-water rivers, flooded forests
Distribution	South America
Length	11 to 13 in.
Weight	Up to 7.5 lb.
Life span	Up to 10 years
Predators	Humans, crocodiles, caiman, larger fish

Diet This piranha eats fish, insects, crustaceans, mollusks, fruit and aquatic plants. When food is scarce, it will take a bite out of a fellow piranha.

Fact This fish has strong jaws, a blunt snout and sharp, triangular teeth that interlock. It is unlikely to feed on a human or large animal unless they're already dead.

Conservation status	**Not evaluated**

European Amazon Ant

Polyergus rufescens

Factfile

Habitat	Grasslands, woodlands
Distribution	Europe, western Asia
Length	.2 to .3 in. (worker ants), .3 to .35 in. (queen)
Nest size	3,000 worker ants, 6,000 slave ants, 1 queen
Life span	45 to 60 days (average for worker ants)
Predators	Other insects, spiders, snails, snakes, birds

Diet The European amazon ant, like other ants, is an omnivore and will forage for fruit, seeds, vegetables, other ants and insects, and carrion.

Fact To obtain pupae (that will become workers for its colony), these ants raid other ants' nests, biting off or piercing the head of guard ants with their jaws.

Conservation status	**Not evaluated**

105

Meat Ant
Iridomyrmex purpureus

Factfile

Habitat   Sandy soil forests, water holes, urban areas
Distribution   Australia
Length   .2 to .5 in. (worker ants), .5 in. (queen)
Nest size   11,000 to over 300,000 worker ants, 1 queen
Life span   45 to 60 days (worker ants), to 15 years (queen)
Predators   Various birds, blind snakes, spiders

Diet   The meat ant forages for plant and animal matter. An "army" of these ants can kill prey much larger than itself. A colony can strip a carcass in a few weeks.

Fact   Meat ants can kill young cane toads, a pest species, without being affected by its toxins. A meat ant colony is an oval-shaped mound, 3 to 6 ft. wide.

Conservation status   **Not evaluated**

Burchell's Army Ant
Eciton burchellii

Factfile

Habitat	Heavily forested shady, damp environments
Distribution	Central and South America
Length	.1 to .5 in. (worker ants), not recorded (queen)
Nest size	Over 500,000 worker ants, 1 queen
Life span	45 to 60 days (worker ants), several years (queen)
Predators	Birds, mammals

Diet A million-strong army of these ants will cover an animal, cut off small pieces and take them to the nest. The prey is basically "eaten" alive.

Fact These ants eat all the prey in an area which is why they have no fixed nests. Ants inject prey with formic acid to damage the prey's circulatory system.

Conservation status　　　　**Not evaluated**

107

Asian Giant Hornet

Vespa mandarinia

Predators

Invertebrates

Hornets

Factfile

Habitat	Low mountains, forested areas
Distribution	Eastern and southeastern Asia
Length	Up to 1.5 in. (workers), 2.2 in. (queen)
Nest size	700 workers
Life span	3 to 5 months (workers), up to 1 year (queen)
Predators	Honey buzzards

Diet This hornet preys on honeybees, mantises and other hornets. It feeds honey larvae to its young. One hornet can kill up to 40 honeybees in 30 seconds.

Fact The .25 inch-long stinger of a giant hornet has 8 chemicals, one which attracts more hornets to the victim. It can't eat solids, so drinks only the prey's fluids.

Conservation status   **Not evaluated**

Antlion (Larva)

Myrmeleon formicariu

Factfile

Habitat	Dry, sandy landscapes
Distribution	Worldwide
Length	.6 in. (larvae), 1.8 in. (adults)
Wingspan	.8 to 4.3 in. (adults only)
Life span	30 to 90 days (larvae), 2 to 3 years (full life cycle)
Predators	No natural predators (larvae)

Diet The antlion larva eats insects, mostly ants, and spiders. It digs a 2 in. pit, buries itself at the base, its mandibles exposed, and waits for prey to fall in.

Fact This large-jawed insect is also called a doodlebug, as it leaves doodle-like trails in the sand. Its mandibles inject a venom to immobilize the prey.

Conservation status	Not evaluated

Assassin Bugs

Reduviidae family

Predators

Invertebrates

True bugs

Factfile

Habitat   Rain forests, urban areas
Distribution   Worldwide
Length   .15 to 1.6 in.
Wingspan   1.6 in.
Life span   1 to 2 years (in captivity)
Predators   Birds, rodents, praying mantises, spiders

Diet Predatory assassin bugs ambush insects, spiders and other true bugs. They stab prey with their curved rostrum (beak) and inject a lethal saliva.

Fact The saliva of these bugs paralyzes their prey. They can kill a cockroach in 4 seconds! To attract a bee, some bugs cover their legs with tree sap.

Conservation status	**Not evaluated**

Water Scorpion

Nepa cinerea

Factfile

Habitat	Still, weedy shallow ponds, stagnant water
Distribution	Britain, Central Europe
Length	.7 to 1 in. plus tail
Wingspan	1 to 1.4 in.
Life span	Up to 7 months
Predators	Large larvae, fish, ducks, leeches, frogs

Diet The water scorpion hides among water plants, grabs its prey, such as water beetles, larvae, tadpoles and fish, stabs it and sucks its fluids.

Fact This bug's whippy tail allows it to breathe when underwater. Like the land scorpion, its front pincer legs are designed for catching and holding prey.

Conservation status   **Not evaluated**

111

Tiger Beetle

Cosmodela aurulenta juxtata

Predators

Invertebrates

Beetles

Factfile

Habitat   Sandy shorelines, mangroves, forest trails
Distribution   Eastern Asia, southeast Asia
Length   .6 to .7 in.
Wingspan   Wings are fused together
Life span   6 weeks
Predators   Dragonflies, robber flies, birds, small vertebrates

Diet The tiger beetle runs down insects and spiders at 5.5 mph. It dismembers them and fills the sections with an enzyme that turns prey into a "smoothie."

Fact Because this beetle's eyes can't produce sharp images quickly while it runs, it sometimes stops the chase for a bit in order to locate the prey again.

Conservation status   **Not evaluated**

Common Whitetail

Plathemis lydia

Factfile

Habitat	Lakes, ponds, slow-moving streams, marshes
Distribution	North America
Length	1.5 to 2 in.
Wingspan	2.5 to 3 in.
Life span	36 days (adult)
Predators	Birds, frogs, other insect eaters

Diet This dragonfly eats flying insects, such as mosquitoes, gnats, flies and smaller dragonflies. It catches them midair with its front legs.

Fact The whitetail is a perching insect. It will rest on rocks and logs while patrolling its stretch of water to expel intruding male whitetails.

Conservation status   **Not evaluated**

113

European Mantis

Mantis religiosa

Factfile

Habitat	Savannahs, grasslands, forests
Distribution	Europe, Asia, Africa, North America
Length	3 to 3.1 in.
Wingspan	2.75 in.
Life span	Up to 1 year
Predators	Frogs, rodents, birds, bats

Diet A mantis eats all day. It ambushes or sneaks up on flies, beetles, caterpillars, bees, butterflies, some moths and even small reptiles, birds and mammals.

Fact The front legs of this insect have sharp spines that grip the prey while it bites its head off. It can catch and eat as many as 16 crickets in a day.

Conservation status	**Least concern**

114

Fringed Jumping Spider

Portia fimbriata

Factfile

Habitat	Tropical rain forests, woodlands, grasslands
Distribution	Northern Australia, southeast Asia
Length	.2 to .4 in. (body)
Weight	.07 oz. (estimate)
Life span	1 year
Predators	Ants, birds, frogs, mantises

Diet This jumping spider eats mostly other spiders, their eggs and insects. It leaps on its prey with fangs extended, injects a lethal venom and eats its catch.

Fact With its coloring, bumpy, tough skin and rest pose (fangs and legs tucked in), this spider can be next to its prey, without the prey even realizing it.

Conservation status	**Not evaluated**

Ant-mimicking Jumping Spider

Myrmarachne maxillosa

Factfile

Habitat	Shrubs in tropical and temperate forests
Distribution	Southeast Asia, southern China
Size	.22 to .31 in. (body)
Weight	.07 oz. (estimate)
Life span	1 to 3 years (estimate)
Predators	Ant-eating insects, mammals and spiders

Diet This jumping spider preys on other spiders and insects, but it is thought that it also eats pollen and nectar. It is a patient and cunning predator.

Fact These spiders imitate ants by waving their long, thin forelegs to mimic ant antennae. This reduces their chance of being eaten by many predators.

Conservation status   **Not evaluated**

Goliath Bird-eating Tarantula
Theraphosa blondi

Factfile

Habitat	Rain forests
Distribution	Northern South America
Size	3 in (body), up to 11 in. (leg span)
Weight	Up to 6.2 oz.
Life span	Up to 20 years (females), 3 to 6 years (males)
Predators	Other tarantulas, spider wasps, snakes, humans

Diet This spider rarely eats birds, preferring insects, earthworms, frogs, snakes, lizards and rodents. It injects its venom with a pair of 1 in. fangs.

Fact The bird-eating tarantula spins a web at the entrance to its burrow. When prey cross it, vibrations bring the spider rushing out to snatch the prey.

Conservation status	**Not evaluated**

Brazilian Black Velvet Tarantula

Grammostola pulchra

Predators

Invertebrates

Spiders

Factfile

Habitat	Grasslands, forests
Distribution	Brazil and Uruguay
Size	2.8 in. (body), 7 in. (leg span)
Weight	Not recorded
Life span	Up to 20 years (females), 6 to 7 years (males)
Predators	Snakes, birds, humans

Diet The Brazilian black velvet tarantula ambush-hunts large insects, such as beetles and crickets, and lizards, young mice and mealworms.

Fact This velvety-smooth spider would rather hide in a burrow than fight. It fasts for 2 to 3 months a year. Many of them are caught and sold as pets.

Conservation status	**Not evaluated**

Mexican Redknee Tarantula

Euathlus smithi

Factfile

Habitat	Scrubland, deserts, dry thorn or tropical forests
Distribution	Central Pacific coast of Mexico
Size	4 in. (body), 6 in. (leg span)
Weight	Up to 3 oz.
Life span	10 to 30 years (females), 5 to 6 years (males)
Predators	Birds, moths, lizards

Diet This spider ambush-hunts small frogs, lizards and mice. Its venom paralyzes the prey and starts the process of turning the prey's tissues into a liquid.

Fact The tips of its legs detect vibrations, smells and tastes. To defend itself, it scrapes hairs off its abdomen towards the threat, which causes blindness.

Conservation status   **Near threatened**

Brazilian Wandering Spider

Phoneutria fera

Factfile

Habitat	Rain forests, urban areas
Distribution	Brazil
Size	2 in. (body), up to 6 in. (leg span)
Weight	3.8 oz.
Life span	1 to 2 years
Predators	Tarantula hawk wasps, rodents, birds

Diet This spider will hunt almost anything as long as it is not too large, such as other spiders and small amphibians, reptiles and mammals, especially mice.

Fact One of the world's most venomous, the wandering spider does not build nests. It actively hunts, using its speed, size and venom to subdue its prey.

Conservation status   **Not evaluated**

Giant Carolina Wolf Spider

Hogna carolinensis

Factfile

Habitat	Deserts, pastures, glades, fields
Distribution	North America
Size	7 to 14 in. (body)
Weight	Not recorded
Life span	Up to 2 years
Predators	Lizards, birds, some rodents

Diet The wolf spider hunts at night and chases down its prey of large insects, such as grasshoppers, crickets and other agricultural pests, and small rodents.

Fact It is not this spider's venom that does it for its prey but the damage done by its bite. With the prey subdued, the spider rolls onto its back and eats.

Conservation status	**Not evaluated**

121

Giant Pacific Octopus

Enteroctopus dofleini

Predators

Invertebrates

Octopuses

Factfile

Habitat	Coastal waters
Distribution	Northern Pacific Ocean
Size	10 to 16.5 ft. (average arm span)
Weight	22 to 110 lb.
Life span	3 to 5 years
Predators	Harbor seals, sea otters, sperm whales, sharks

Diet The giant Pacific octopus forages and hunts for shrimp, clams, lobsters, fish and their eggs, crabs, abalone, scallops, octopuses and even sharks.

Fact The intelligent giant's arms have up to 280 suckers each. Its grip is almost inescapable. The largest specimen caught had an arm span of 30 feet.

Conservation status   **Not evaluated**

Bigfin Reef Squid

Sepioteuthis lessoniana

Factfile

Habitat	Warm coastal waters
Distribution	Indian and Pacific Oceans
Length	1.5 to 13 in.
Weight	.9 to 4.8 lb.
Life span	4 to 6 months
Predators	Tuna, marlin, oval squid

Diet This squid ambushes fish, mollusks and crustaceans. It eats up to sixty percent of its body weight a day, so it needs to a catch a fish every 2 hours.

Fact A bigfin squid floats upright below its prey before trapping it in its two long tentacles. Its beak (mouth) and tongue cut and grind the food.

Conservation status   Not evaluated

Lion's Mane Jellyfish

Cyanea capillata

Predators

Invertebrates

Jellyfish

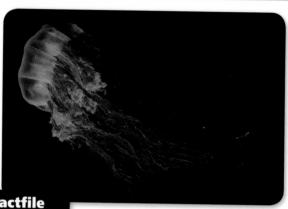

Factfile

Habitat   Cooler open oceans
Distribution   Northern Atlantic and Pacific Oceans, North Sea
Size   Up to 6.5 ft. (bell), up to 100 ft. (tentacles)
Weight   Up to 485 lb.
Life span   1 year
Predators   Leatherback turtles, birds, ocean sunfish

Diet The lion's mane eats fish, plankton and other jellyfish. Once prey is stung by its tentacles, it is paralyzed. It is then torn into pieces and eaten.

Fact This jellyfish's body is 95% water, and has between 560 to 1,200 tentacles. The largest specimen ever found was 7.5 ft. across with 120 ft. long tentacles.

Conservation status   **Not evaluated**

Mottled Pistol Shrimp

Alpheus bidens

Factfile

Habitat   Coral reefs, seagrass beds
Distribution Indian and west Pacific Oceans
Length   Up to 3 in. (body)
Weight   Not recorded
Life span   Up to 4 years
Predators   Larger fish

Diet This shrimp fires a 62 mph bubble bullet of water at small fish, crabs and worms rendering them senseless or dead. It drags prey back to its burrow.

Fact The pistol shrimp's bullets are produced by a compression plunger in its huge snapper claw, creating one of the loudest noises in the sea.

Conservation status   **Not evaluated**

125

Glossary

Ambush To hide and wait for prey to come near.

Amphibian A vertebrate animal, such as frogs, newts, toads and salamanders.

Apex predator An animal at the top of its food chain that has no predators in its ecosystem.

Bait ball Formed when small fish mass into a small, packed area as a defense against a predator.

Baleen whale A whale that filters food from water.

Camouflage Coloring or texture that blends with the surroundings.

Canine teeth Sharp-pointed teeth, on either side of the upper and lower jaw, meant for grasping and tearing food.

Carcass Body of a dead animal.

Carrion Remains of dead animals.

Cartilaginous Having a skeleton of cartilage not bone. Sharks, rays and dogfish are cartilaginous fish.

Cephalopod A type of mollusk including octopuses, squid, cuttlefish and nautilus.

Crustacean A type of arthropod that includes crabs, lobsters, shrimp and krill.

Feces Excreted solid waste.

Falconry Training falcons or other birds of prey to hunt and return.

Filter feed To strain food, like plankton, from water.

Forage To search for food.

Grassland An open area covered mostly with grass.

Hibernation Spending winter in a deep sleep.

Ice floe A sheet of floating ice.

Invasive An animal that increases its population in a new habitat.

Invertebrate An animal without a backbone including crabs, snails and octopuses.

Juvenile A young animal.

Krill A small, shrimplike plankton found in all oceans.

Larva The young of an animal, especially insects.

Mandibles A pair of appendages near the mouth of an insect used for grasping and cutting food.

Mammal A warm-blooded vertebrate animal with hair or fur that has live young fed by milk.

Marsupial A mammal that gives birth to tiny, underdeveloped young that grow inside a pouch.

Mollusk A soft-bodied animal without a backbone, including snails, mussels and squid.

Omnivore An animal that feeds on plant and animal matter.

Opportunistic An animal that exploits any food options.

Opossum An American marsupial.

Pectoral fins Two fins on either side of a fish's head.

Plumage The patterns, colors and arrangement of feathers covering a bird.

Prairie An expansive plain of land covered mainly by grass.

Predator An animal that kills and eats other animals.

Primate A mammal, such as apes, monkeys, lemurs and humans.

Pupa A stage of an insect's life.

Raptor A bird of prey, such as eagles and hawks.

Regurgitate The act of bringing food that has been swallowed back to and out of the mouth.

Reptile A vertebrate, such as snakes, lizards, crocodiles, turtles and tortoises.

Rodent A mammal, such as rats, mice, squirrels and porcupines.

Rookery A breeding colony.

Saliva A liquid produced by glands that is used to aid chewing and swallowing.

Savannah A grass plain in tropical areas, especially in Africa.

Scavenger An animal that feeds on refuse and other decaying organic matter.

Serrated Jagged, sawlike teeth.

Shoal A mass of fish moving together.

Songbird Any perching bird that sings.

Stalk To follow an animal without that animal knowing it.

Talon A claw.

Temperate An area where temperatures do not get too high or too low.

Territorial An animal that remains in and defends its "home."

Tropical water Constantly warm water found between the tropics of Cancer and Capricorn.

Tunicate An invertebrate filter feeder like a sea squirt.

Vertebrate An animal with a backbone, such as mammals, birds, reptiles, amphibians and fish.

Index